Soups! Weight Loss Miracle in a Bowl

Julia Cussler

Diet Recipe Books – Healthy Cooking for Healthy Living

ISBN-13: 978-1508716525

ISBN-10: 1508716528

Copyright © 2014 by IVlassov Publishing. All rights reserved worldwide.

No part of this publication may be replicated, redistributed, or given away in any form without the prior written consent of the author/publisher.

All information in this book has been researched and checked for factual accuracy. However, the authors and publishers provide no warranty, express or implied, that the information contained herein is appropriate for every individual, situation or purpose, and assume no responsibility for errors or omissions. The reader assumes the risk and full responsibility for all actions, and the authors will not be held responsible for any loss or damage, whether consequential, incidental, and special or otherwise that in any way connected with the information presented in this book.

Books by Julia Cussler

Juicing for Health

Quick and Easy Soup Recipes

Vegetarian Slow Cooker Recipes

Natural Cholesterol Solution

Table of Contents

Slim Down with Delicious Soups 7
What is Behind the "Cabbage Soup Diet" 9
The Dangers of Fast Weight Loss 11
Health Benefits of Soup 13
How to Create a Healthy Diet Plan 21
What to Look for in a Diet Plan 24
What are the Healthiest Soups 28
Tips to Make Soup Work for You 30
Soup Recipes for Healthy Weight Loss 33
Black Bean Soup 34
Apple Butternut Squash Soup 36
Simple Stovetop Chicken Noodle Soup 38
Low-Calorie Salsa Soup 40
Hearty Root Vegetable Soup 42
Creamy Onion Soup 44
Cauliflower Cheese Soup 46
Hearty Lentil Soup 48
Vegetarian Chickpea Soup 50
Fast and Easy Minestrone Soup 52
Wild Rice and Mushroom Soup 54
Light Split Pea Soup with Ham 56

Low-Calorie Garden Vegetable Soup 58

Low-Calorie Mexican Fiesta Soup 60

Healthy Asian Twist Soup 62

Chicken Soup with Mushrooms 64

Cream of Broccoli Soup 66

High-Fiber Lentil Soup 68

Arugula Detoxification Soup 70

Hearty Meatball Soup 72

Quick and Easy Broccoli Soup 74

Carrot and Rice Soup 76

Cabbage Soup 78

Chicken and Noodles Soup 80

Avocado and Cauliflower Soup 82

Green Power Soup 84

Tomato Soup 86

Smoky Corn Soup 88

Cauliflower and Avocado Soup 90

Carrot and Ginger Soup 92

Green Veggie Medley Soup 94

Savory Tortilla Soup 96

Gran's Lentil Soup 98

Light Roasted Red Pepper Soup 100

Rich Tom Yum Soup 102

Classic Chicken Soup 104

Beets with Horseradish Borscht 106

Tomato Spinach Delight 108

Hot Vegetable Soup 110

Tofu Udon Soup 112

Low Calorie Bloody Mary Soup..................................114

Mushroom and Barley Marmite 116

Turkey Jerky Garlic Soup 118

Northwestern Lentil Chili Soup 120

Healthy Taco Soup...122

Classic Eggplant Soup 124

"Red Tide" Soup 126

Chicken Asparagus Pottage......................................128

Chicken-Parsnip Pea Soup 130

Green Velvet Pea Soup..132

Fresh Asparagus Chicken Soup.................................134

Cool Pea and Mint Soup...136

Meatball Escarole Soup..138

Homemade Tomato Gazpacho 140

Spicy Soup: "Aunt Love"..142

From the Author..145

Slim Down with Delicious Soups

When you decided to read this book, what did you hope to get out of the experience? Maybe you have a substantial amount of weight to lose or are concerned with improving your overall health and well-being. Maybe you've heard about particular soups that are supposed to lead to weight loss, such as cabbage soup. Perhaps you already love eating soup and have wondered if there is a way to make it work for your health improvement.

Soup does have the power to improve your overall health and boost your weight loss efforts, but there are many myths floating around the Internet that may lead you in the wrong direction. If you want to get the most out of soup and learn how to make soups that fit your healthy diet, you need to bust those myths and learn the facts about this nutritious food option.

Soups are just like salads: everybody considers them very healthy, but you can easily eliminate all healthy benefits if you add the wrong ingredients. Drench a vegetable salad with creamy, high-fat dressings, and you add calories and unhealthy fat that sabotage your health and fitness goals despite the nutritious benefits of the vegetables. The same problem surfaces when you add high-fat ingredients to your soups. So, as simple as it looks, soup requires careful consideration when you use it as a weight loss tool.

If you use it right, soup will help you to stay healthy, nourish your body, increase your energy levels, and basically help your body thrive and heal. Soup is an amazing resource for those who are focused on fitness and health, so get ready to think of this delicious food in a new light.

What is Behind the "Cabbage Soup Diet"

Many people start thinking about soup as a weight loss tool when they hear about the Cabbage Soup Diet. This diet is also known as the Kick Start Soup Diet or the 7-Day Soup Diet. There are a variety of plans and recipes for this diet online, but the concept is usually the same:

- You follow a recipe to make a special cabbage soup.

- You consume that soup at every meal for one week.
- You consume only a few other foods each day or even no other food at all.

In most cases, the foods that you can eat in addition to the cabbage soup are selective, and you can only have small amounts of those foods. The majority of your nutrition, or lack thereof, comes from the cabbage soup. You can find a variety of recipes for the soup online and in some diet books, but the main ingredient always is the cabbage.

Do you lose weight on the Cabbage Soup Diet? Yes, you can lose up to 25 pounds in just one week with this diet. That sounds great until you learn the real reasons that you see that weight loss on the scale. For starters, you won't lose up to 25 pounds of stored body fat. You lose fluids and possibly even some muscle mass if you follow this strict diet for a long period of time or if you follow the diet without an interval at least three weeks between diet weeks.

Don't get me wrong, I'm not against the cabbage soup, I'm against extreme dieting and fasting that can cause serious health problems.

The Dangers of Fast Weight Loss

Even if you could maintain the weight you lost while on the Cabbage Soup Diet, there are consequences to taking the pounds off too quickly. For one, you are more likely to burn lean muscle tissue rather than fat. Less muscle means you burn fewer calories on a daily basis, which works against you when trying to maintain your weight loss. You may also develop gallstones and suffer other physical ailments if you lose weight too rapidly.

Since the cabbage soup does not provide all of the nutrients that the human body needs to live healthfully, your body is not properly nourished when you follow this diet. The lack of nutritional balance combined with drastically low caloric intake is the reason this is a one-week diet. It is not healthy to put your body through that stress.

Even though long-term weight loss from the Cabbage Soup Diet is very questionable, soup is still a Weight Loss Miracle in a Bowl if you use it carefully as part of a serious and balanced diet. There are still many benefits of consuming soup when you need to lose weight or want to improve your overall health. The next chapters will help you understand these benefits while learning how to implement soup in your healthy lifestyle.

Health Benefits of Soup

You aren't going to get long-term results from the Cabbage Soup Diet or any other extreme diet that's not sustainable over the long-term. The good news is that soup is tremendously health beneficial when used appropriately. Better yet, some soup recipes contain all of the nutrients you need to remain energetic, focused, and healthy in your daily life. You can use soup to achieve all of the following:

- Control hunger between meals.
- Reduce your calories without feeling deprived.
- Enjoy your favorite flavors without taking in a ton of calories.
- Enjoy delicious food while trying to lose body weight.
- Lose body fat rather than water weight or muscle tissue.

If you enjoy eating and can never stick with diets due to the small portion sizes, soup may fit your lifestyle and personality perfectly. You can consume a greater amount of soup without taking in excessive calories, especially if you keep the ingredients in the soup low calorie, high fiber, and nutrient dense. The healthiest soups include all of the following:

- Carbohydrates
- Healthy fats
- Protein
- Fiber
- Vitamins
- Minerals

Your body needs all of these elements to remain healthy and sustain its energy levels, and you can get them all if you implement low-calorie, delicious soups into your balanced long-term diet.

The Benefits of Fiber

Soup is a high-fiber food, and that works to your advantage when trying to lose weight. You can get fiber from the vegetables in a soup, and some soups have high-fiber grains like barley and brown rice, as well. When looking at soup recipes, always use the highest-fiber option when selecting ingredients. For instance, you can use whole grain brown rice instead of white rice because white rice has been stripped of its natural fiber.

The more fiber you include in your diet, the fuller you should feel between meals. You can eat less of a high-fiber meal and feel fuller longer than you would with a larger portion of a low-fiber meal. Fiber also helps your digestive track function properly, so waste is processed out of your body more efficiently and you don't experience as much gas and bloating.

Fill Up without the Fat

Another benefit of soup is that it helps you feel fuller between meals without providing large amounts of unhealthy fats. If you prepare your soup with olive oil or other healthy fats, you can boost your energy levels tremendously without taking in a ton of fatty calories. Keep this in mind as you start browsing soup recipes.

Some studies have shown that people who consume soup at the start of a meal consume approximately 100 fewer calories over the course of the meal than those who do not consume soup at the start of the meal. You can also expect to consume fewer calories and experience fewer food cravings between meals. This is especially true for high-fiber, low-fat soups.

The Convenience of Soup

You can make a large batch of soup and keep it in the kitchen for those times when you're hungry but don't have the time or energy to prepare a healthy meal. You can even take soup with you to ensure that you always have a healthy meal on hand when you are at work or on the go. All you need is a spoon and a way to heat the soup up.

Consistency Counts

These benefits to consuming soup while losing weight are impressive, but you won't get the results you want or expect without consistency on your part. You need to develop a healthy eating plan that supports your body as it starts to burn off the stored body fat, and then you need to stick with that eating plan over the long term.

This means sticking with your diet even when you are craving unhealthy foods or when the stress of life gets you down. There will always be difficult times when you want to forget about your healthy soup and comfort yourself with some of your favorite fatty foods. That is when you will need to focus on your goals and remind yourself why you turned to soup and why you wanted to lose weight in the beginning.

If you do slip up and consume unhealthy foods, you can easily get right back on track by making a big pot of your favorite soup and allowing it to nourish your body.

How to Create a Healthy Diet Plan

Now that you know the truth about the Cabbage Soup Diet, you are probably wondering whether there are any healthy and well-balanced diet plans that allow you to enjoy soup on a routine basis. Since every human body is different, I strongly recommend you get help from a professional dietitian or bariatrician for developing a weight loss plan or diet that is specially designed for you and takes into account all aspects of your personal health situation. You will certainly maximize your benefits in the long term if you follow a diet that was designed for you by a medical professional who is familiar with your body and health history.

With the help of a professional, you need to determine the following:

- What is your healthy weight and what do you need to lose?
- How many calories do you need to consume daily for a healthy weight loss process according to your lifestyle?
- What amount of nutrients does your body need to consume daily to ensure healthy weight loss?
- How will your medical history and your current health conditions affect your diet plan? (This is why I can't recommend to you any particular diet plan inside this book; nobody can do it without knowing your medical history and your current health conditions.)
- On what kind of healthy food should your meal plan be based (considering what foods you love and which ones you don't)?
- What unhealthy habits you have and how can you gradually reduce or completely eliminate them? No overnight radical changes should be made.
- What eating schedule do you prefer? (How many meals a day is comfortable for you?)

- Are you going to exercise? It seems like a strange question, but please set realistic goals; if you are going to take a 20-minute walk instead of doing an hour-long intense workout, your diet plan has to be adjusted accordingly.
- What kind of weight loss diet plan are you going to choose? This is where you should really take into consideration a balanced, soup-based diet.
- How long do you need to follow this diet plan? Another strange question. This healthy diet plan should become a part of your lifestyle. So, the answer is forever!

You can choose from many healthy diet plans that lean heavily on soup. These diets incorporate the soup along with other healthy foods that provide nutrients and calories needed to sustain energy levels and support weight loss. They also incorporate a different soup each day, so you are always eating different flavors and textures. This ensures that you don't get bored eating the same soup over and over again.

What to Look for in a Diet Plan

Before you commit to a weight loss or health plan, ask yourself whether you can realistically follow that plan for a long period of time. If the plan recommends that you follow the diet for only a week or a month and then resume your old eating habits for a period of time before trying it again, you can guarantee that it is not healthy. You should be able to follow your plan for months on end without any consequences other than healthy weight loss, improved energy levels, and a healthier body inside and out.

Your diet plan should also incorporate different types of soups and other foods that you enjoy eating. Have you ever tried to live on cottage cheese, baked chicken breasts, and other dry, bland diet foods? If so, you know that those diets never last long term, and you end up gaining all of that lost weight back. You don't want that to happen, so make sure you can consume a variety of soups with flavors you enjoy.

Finally, make sure your soup diet plan does not require you to cut out entire food groups or types of food. For example, you know that some fats are healthy, so don't let a diet book or plan convince you that all types of fat will lead to a bubble butt, thunder thighs, or belly flab. The same goes for diet plans that turn carbohydrates into the enemy. It is all about selecting the healthiest fats and whole grain carbohydrates loaded with fiber and other nutrients.

Here is an example of a well-balanced one-day meal plan that I created for myself based on 1,300 daily caloric intake recommended by my dietitian. Note that every single day contains a different soup for lunch. Sometimes when I am really hungry, I also have soup for a snack or dinner, because due to its low calorie volume, it doesn't affect the totally allowed calories.

Breakfast

- Nordica 1% low-fat cottage cheese, 125 g (1/2 cup) (100 cal)
- Green salad with mixed raw vegetables, 2 cups (44 cal)
- 1 cup of Tetley Classic Green Tea, 1 bag (0 cal)
- Bread - Whole-wheat, toasted, 1 slice (69 cal)

Total: 213 calories

Snack

- Apple - raw, with skin, 1 medium (2-3/4") (72 cal)
- 1 green bell pepper Gladys (30 cal)

Total: 102 calories

Lunch

- 1 cup carrot and rice soup (160 cal)
- turkey breast, oven roasted, extra lean, 55 g (3 slices) (60 cal)
- 1 medium baked potato (129 cal)

Total: 349 calories

Snack

Generic fruit salad, cantaloupe, honeydew, grapes, watermelon, pineapple, 1 cup (80 cal)

Yogurt - plain, low fat (1% fat), 1 cup (8 oz.) (154 cal)

Total: 234 calories

Dinner

- Fish - Atlantic salmon, farm raised, grilled/baked/broiled, 4 oz. cooked (232 cal)
- Large green salad with mixed raw vegetables, 5 cups with low fat dressing (110 cal).

Total: 342

What are the Healthiest Soups

There are many different types of soup, and the healthiest ones are those that pile on the fiber and nutrients without adding a lot of fat to the recipe. This means you should typically choose soups that are water or broth based over those that are have a base of heavy cream. Vegetable soup is one of the best soups out there because it is packed with high-fiber vegetables; you can cook it with healthy olive oil, and it does not include high-fat meats that add too much to the fat and calorie content of the soup overall.

You can also keep your soups on the light side by focusing on whole grains rather than refined white grains. Always go with whole grain rice, barley, and other grains that have not been stripped of their original fiber. When you strip the color, you strip the nutrients and fiber.

What about Sodium

Sodium is probably the biggest concern when it comes to soup, especially if you choose canned soups or use canned broth. If you are willing to make your own soup at home, you can cut back on the sodium considerably. Look out for low-sodium vegetables if you buy them canned and avoid adding salt into the soup. Some recipes will call for salt, but you don't have to put as much in your soup as the recipe suggests.

Tips to Make Soup Work for You

All weight loss tools can become unhealthy if they are used in the wrong way. Soup is a powerful tool for weight loss. To maximize the benefits of soup in your diet and make sure you're using it in a healthy manner at all times, consider these 11 tips for using soup successfully.

1. Don't expect to eat only soup for a long period of time. This gets boring and is unhealthy even when the soup is full of high-quality ingredients. You will only set yourself up for failure if you eliminate all other foods.
2. Don't add high-fat ingredients to your soup. Why ruin a good thing?
3. Once you find a soup you like, make adjustments to create additional recipes from the original. You can switch the recommended vegetables, add whole grain rice or pasta, or alter the spices to create new flavors.
4. Although soup does contain water, continue to drink water between meals. Dehydration will interfere with your weight loss efforts.
5. Try to use low-sodium broths and canned vegetables whenever possible. You can also use frozen vegetables to cut down on sodium. Sodium may lead to high blood pressure and may increase bloating and swelling. Fresh vegetables and homemade broth are the best low-sodium solutions.
6. Don't drink extra calories when trying to lose weight. It's okay if you want to tip up your bowl and suck down every last drop of your soup, but stay away from high-calorie sodas and juices. Pure water for a drink is your best bet during the weight loss process.
7. Keep a collection of soup recipes that you enjoy. Variety is the spice of life, and you don't want to get tired of your favorites.

8. Make large batches of soup and freeze individual servings. This is an easy way to create your own microwave meals. When you are pressed for time, you always have something healthy to grab before you run out of the house.
9. Use fresh ingredients in your soups whenever possible. Shop for organic produce through local farmers' markets whenever possible. These vegetables will have the most nutrients with the fewest chemicals.
10. Many soup recipes in this book are based on chicken broth. You can use canned stock, like Campbell's Low Sodium Chicken Broth, but it is advisable that you prepare your own homemade stock. It is really easy to do; you just boil a whole chicken in a big pot with a couple of onions, 2 carrots, and 2 celery stalks for 30–40 minutes. Add salt and pepper to taste, and don't forget you are making this homemade broth to avoid high sodium content, so be careful with salt. Take out the chicken meat for future use and get rid of the vegetables. You can then freeze the stock for future use.
11. Think of soup as a tool to help you lose weight and stay healthy. This is not a diet that you are going to quit as soon as you reach your target weight. This is a lifestyle change that will ensure you live as healthfully as possible for the rest of your life.

Soup Recipes for Healthy Weight Loss

Are you ready to start making soup at home and experimenting with the benefits of using soup to maintain your weight and stay healthy? The following recipes are all reasonably low in calories, and many are extremely low. They all contain healthy fats and a variety of vegetables and grains that will help you stay healthy, trim, and energetic.

Black Bean Soup

Ingredients:

- 1 onion, chopped
- 4 garlic cloves, minced
- 1 tablespoon cumin
- 2 tablespoons olive oil
- 1 medium carrot, chopped
- ½ lime

- 1 cup chicken broth
- 3 cups fresh tomato, chopped
- 15 oz. canned black beans, low sodium
- 1.4 oz. canned green chili peppers, diced (optional)
- Tortilla chips

Directions:

1. Sauté chopped onion, minced garlic, cumin, and olive oil.
2. Add chicken broth, fresh tomato, canned black beans, carrot, and canned green chili peppers and bring to a boil.
3. Simmer over low heat for 15 minutes.
4. Serve with tortilla chips and lime.

Recipe makes 4 servings; 195 calories per serving.

Apple Butternut Squash Soup

Ingredients:

- 2 lb. halved lengthwise butternut squash
- 1 tablespoon olive oil
- ½ red onion, chopped
- 3 apples, peeled and diced
- ½ cube vegetarian bouillon
- ¼ cup fresh ginger, grated
- ¼ teaspoon ground nutmeg
- 2 cups water
- ½ cup skim milk
- ½ teaspoon salt
- ½ teaspoon ground pepper

Directions:
1. Preheat oven to 400° F.
2. Place butternut squash in a baking dish with the hollow side facing down.
3. Cover the butternut squash with foil and bake for 45 minutes, until tender. Allow to cool while continuing to follow steps.
4. Heat olive oil over low heat in a large saucepan.
5. Add onion to the olive oil and cook eight minutes, stirring occasionally.
6. Add apples, vegetarian bouillon cube, ginger, nutmeg, and water to the olive oil mixture. Bring to a boil over high heat.
7. Reduce saucepan heat to low and simmer for 10 minutes. Remove saucepan from the heat.
8. Remove the flesh from the inside of the squash shells.
9. Puree squash flesh with the milk and put into a bowl.
10. Puree half of the apple mixture until it has a smooth texture and place back in the saucepan.
11. Add squash puree to the saucepan.
12. Mix apple and squash purees, adding milk if necessary to create a smooth texture.
13. Simmer the saucepan over low heat for approximately 10 minutes, stirring occasionally.
14. Add salt and pepper to your taste.

Recipe makes 4 servings; 196 calories per serving.

Simple Stovetop Chicken Noodle Soup

Ingredients:

- 3 cups chicken broth
- 1 carrot, chopped
- 1 stalk celery, chopped
- ½ cup egg noodles, uncooked
- 1 cup cooked chicken, cubed

Directions:

1. Combine chicken broth, celery, and carrot in a large saucepan. Bring to a boil.
2. Add egg noodles and cooked chicken to the saucepan.
3. Cook on medium heat for 10–15 minutes.
4. Remove saucepan from heat and serve with parsley leaves on top.

Recipe makes 4 servings; 140 calories per serving.

Low-Calorie Salsa Soup

Ingredients:

- 1 tablespoon olive oil
- 1 tablespoon minced garlic
- 2 cups water
- ½ teaspoon chipotle chili powder

- 15 oz. canned black beans, drained and rinsed
- 8 oz. salsa
- 1 tablespoon lime juice
- 1 cup cilantro, chopped

Directions:

1. Heat oil in a large saucepan over medium heat.
2. Add garlic to the saucepan and sauté for one minute.
3. Add water, chipotle chili powder, beans, and salsa to the saucepan and bring to a boil.
4. Reduce heat on the saucepan and simmer for one minute.
5. Blend three cups of the black bean mixture in a blender or food processor until it has a smooth texture. Return pureed mixture to the saucepan.
6. Add lime juice to the saucepan and simmer for 10 minutes.
7. Remove saucepan from heat and add cilantro.

Recipe makes 4 servings; 153 calories per serving.

Hearty Root Vegetable Soup

Ingredients:

- 3 cups baked potato, peeled and chopped
- 2 ½ cups turnips, peeled and chopped
- 1 ½ cups rutabaga, peeled and chopped
- 1 ¼ cups butternut squash, peeled and chopped
- 1 cup onion, chopped

- 1 cup carrot, chopped
- 1 ½ teaspoon dried rubbed sage
- ¼ teaspoon salt
- 2 cups chicken broth, low sodium, fat-free
- 2 cups 2% low-fat milk

Directions:

1. Mix baked potato, turnips, rutabaga, butternut squash, onion, carrot, dried rubbed sage, salt, and chicken broth in a Dutch oven and bring to a boil.
2. Simmer on low heat for 30 minutes.
3. Remove from heat and allow to rest unheated for 10 minutes.
4. Blend vegetable mixture until smooth in three smaller portions, pouring into a large bowl to blend.
5. Pour blended vegetable mixture to the pan and add milk.
6. Cook vegetable mixture on medium heat until thoroughly heated.

Recipe makes 8 servings; 133 calories per serving.

Creamy Onion Soup

Ingredients:

- 2 ½ lb. sweet onions, peeled and quartered
- 1 head garlic, unpeeled
- 2 ½ cups chicken broth, fat-free, low sodium
- 1 bay leaf
- ¼ cup sherry
- ¼ teaspoon black pepper
- Dash of salt
- 1 teaspoon lemon juice

Directions:

1. Preheat oven to 375° F.
2. Spray a baking sheet with cooking spray and set quartered onion pieces on a baking sheet. Lightly coat the onion quarters with cooking spray.
3. Skin the garlic head, leaving the individual cloves together and unpeeled. Drizzle water over the garlic head, wrap in foil, and place the foil on the baking sheet with the quartered onion pieces.
4. Bake onion pieces and garlic head for 30 minutes. Turn and bake for another 30 minutes.
5. Set onion pieces and garlic out to cool.
6. Place onion quarters in a large saucepan.
7. Take the garlic cloves apart and squeeze pulp into the saucepan. Throw garlic skins away.
8. Add chicken broth, bay leaf, sherry, pepper, and salt to the saucepan. Simmer over low heat for 15 minutes.
9. Discard bay leaf.
10. Blend the mixture until it has a smooth texture and then return it to the saucepan. Heat soup thoroughly over low heat.
11. Add lemon juice.

Recipe makes 4 servings; 141 calories per serving.

Cauliflower Cheese Soup

Ingredients:

- 1 tablespoon olive oil
- 1 white leek, rinsed and sliced
- 1 cup water
- 1 bay leaf
- 1 ¼ cups low-fat milk, divided
- 3 cups fresh cauliflower, chopped
- Dash of salt and pepper
- 1 ½ tablespoons all-purpose flour
- ½ tablespoon lemon juice

Directions:

1. Place olive oil in large saucepan and set to medium heat.
2. Add the white leek to the saucepan and cook for five minutes, stirring occasionally.
3. Add water, bay leaf, cauliflower, salt, pepper, and 1 cup milk to the saucepan and bring to a boil.
4. Simmer approximately 10 minutes, stirring occasionally.
5. Whisk the rest of the milk with the all-purpose flour. Add mixture to the saucepan after it is finished boiling. Remove bay leaf.
6. Cook mixture over medium heat for a couple minutes to thicken the soup.
7. Blend the mixture until it has a smooth texture and return to the saucepan. Heat soup thoroughly over low heat.
8. Add lemon juice and a little dill leaf if desired.

Recipe makes 4 servings; 112 calories per serving.

Hearty Lentil Soup

Ingredients:

- 1 cup brown lentils, rinsed
- 2 cups cold water
- 2 cups vegetable broth
- 1 tablespoon olive oil
- Dash of salt and pepper
- 2 large carrots, chopped
- ½ red onion, diced

- 2 cloves garlic, minced
- 1 teaspoon ground cumin
- 1 ½ tablespoons lemon juice

Directions:

1. Combine brown lentils, water, and vegetable broth in a Dutch oven on high heat. Bring to a boil.
2. Cover lentils and simmer over low heat covered for 30–40 minutes.
3. Place olive oil in large saucepan and heat thoroughly.
4. Combine onion, carrots, salt, and pepper in the saucepan and cook on medium heat for 15 minutes.
5. Add cumin and garlic to the onion mixture and remove saucepan from heat.
6. Add onion mixture and lemon juice to the lentils when the lentils are done cooking. Serve with parsley leaves.

Recipe makes 3 servings; 193 calories per serving.

Vegetarian Chickpea Soup

Ingredients:

- 1 tablespoon olive oil
- 2–3 celery stalks, chopped
- 1 large onion, chopped
- 1 ½ teaspoon ground cumin
- 2 cups vegetable stock

- 2 cups chickpeas, drained
- 2 large tomatoes, chopped
- 2 cups green beans
- 1 tablespoon lemon juice

Directions:

1. In large saucepan, heat the olive oil for a few minutes over medium heat.
2. Add celery and onion to the saucepan and heat for 5 minutes, stirring occasionally.
3. Add cumin to the saucepan and continue cooking for 2 more minutes.
4. Add vegetable stock, chickpeas, and tomatoes to the saucepan and simmer on low heat for 10 minutes.
5. Add green beans and lemon juice to the saucepan and heat thoroughly.

Recipe makes 6 servings; 136 calories per serving.

Fast and Easy Minestrone Soup

Ingredients:

- 4 cups vegetable broth
- 2 cups tomatoes, chopped
- 2 oz. package thin spaghetti noodles
- 3 cups frozen mixed vegetables

- 4 tablespoons pesto
- 1 tablespoon olive oil

Directions:

1. Combine vegetable broth and tomatoes in a large pot and bring to a boil.
2. Break the spaghetti noodles into small pieces and add everything to the pot. Boil until the noodles are almost soft.
3. Add frozen mixed vegetables to the pot and return to a boil.
4. Simmer soup mixture for approximately five minutes to heat thoroughly.

Recipe makes 4 servings; 192 calories per serving.

Wild Rice and Mushroom Soup

Ingredients:

- 1/3 cup wild rice
- 2 cloves garlic, minced
- 2 stalks celery, chopped
- 1 onion, chopped
- Dash of salt and pepper
- 3 cups cauliflower, chopped
- 7 cups water, divided
- ½ teaspoon onion powder
- 1 teaspoon Dijon mustard
- 2 cups mushrooms, chopped
- 1 cup Greek yogurt, fat-free
- 2 tablespoons arrowroot flour
- 1 tablespoon olive oil

Directions:
1. Combine wild rice, two cups of water, and a dash of salt in a small saucepan and bring to a boil.
2. Reduce heat on the rice and simmer for approximately 30 minutes, cooking until tender.
3. Combine garlic, celery, onion, cauliflower, salt, and pepper in a medium saucepan with olive oil and heat for three minutes until soft.
4. Add four cups of water, onion powder, Dijon mustard, and one cup of chopped mushrooms to the saucepan and bring to a boil.
5. Simmer the mixture in the saucepan over low heat for approximately eight minutes while covered. The cauliflower should become tender at this point.
6. Blend the saucepan mixture to obtain a smooth texture and then return the mixture to the saucepan.
7. Add the cooked wild rice and one cup of chopped mushrooms to the saucepan and bring to a boil.
8. Simmer over low heat for approximately five minutes.
9. Combine Greek yogurt, one cup of water, and arrowroot flour in a small mixing bowl; mix well.
10. Add the Greek yogurt mixture to the wild rice mixture and simmer for approximately five minutes.

Recipe makes 4 servings; 148 calories per serving.

Light Split Pea Soup with Ham

Ingredients:

- ½ lb. green split peas
- 8 cups chicken stock
- 1 onion, chopped
- 2 ½ cloves garlic, minced

- 1 teaspoon oregano
- Dash of pepper
- 1 bay leaf
- 2 cups carrots, chopped
- 2 stalks celery, chopped
- 1 cup chopped cooked ham

Directions:

1. Combine green split peas, chicken stock, onion, garlic, oregano, pepper, and bay leaf in a large pot. Simmer for 60 minutes uncovered.
2. Add carrots and celery to the pot and simmer for another 30 minutes.
3. Remove bay leaf from the pot.
4. Blend the soup until it becomes creamy and smooth. Split into small batches if necessary.
5. Return soup to pot and add chopped ham.
6. Simmer for 15 minutes on low heat.

Recipe makes 6 servings; 196 calories per serving.

Low-Calorie Garden Vegetable Soup

Ingredients:

- 1 tablespoon olive oil
- 4 cups vegetable broth
- 1 carrot, peeled and diced
- 2 teaspoon garlic, minced

- 1 medium onion, diced
- 1/2 lb. broccoli
- 1/4 lb. frozen or fresh green beans
- 1 teaspoon dried basil
- 1 teaspoon dried oregano
- 1 teaspoon kosher salt
- 1 medium zucchini, diced
- 2 stalks celery, diced

Directions:

1. Heat oil in a large saucepan over medium heat.
2. Add onion, celery and garlic and cook for 5 minutes.
3. Pour the vegetable broth, add carrot into a saucepan and bring to a boil.
4. Reduce heat and simmer at medium heat for five minutes.
5. Add broccoli, green beans, tomato paste, dried basil, dried oregano, and kosher salt to the saucepan. Bring to a boil.
6. Simmer mixture on medium heat for 20 minutes.
7. Add zucchini and heat until it softens.

Recipe makes 4 servings; 63 calories per serving.

Low-Calorie Mexican Fiesta Soup

Ingredients:

- 3 cups vegetable broth
- 1 can Mexican-style diced tomatoes
- 1 cup fresh or frozen green beans
- 2 cloves garlic, minced
- 1 zucchini, diced

- 1 tomatillo, cubed
- 1 small poblano chili pepper, diced
- 1 small jalapeno pepper, stripped of seeds and membrane
- ½ yellow onion, chopped
- ½ green pepper, chopped
- ½ red pepper, chopped
- ¼ teaspoon cumin
- ¼ teaspoon dried oregano
- Dash of salt
- 1 tablespoon lime juice
- ¼ cup fresh cilantro, chopped

Directions:

1. Place the vegetable broth in a large pot and bring it to a boil.
2. Add diced tomatoes, green beans, zucchini, tomatillo, poblano chili pepper, jalapeno pepper, onion, green pepper, red pepper, cumin, and dried oregano to the pot. Bring to a boil while covered.
3. Partially uncover the pot and simmer over low heat for 10 minutes.
4. Add salt, lime juice, and cilantro.

Recipe makes 6 servings; 54 calories per serving.

Healthy Asian Twist Soup

Ingredients:

- 3 cups vegetable broth
- 1 cup Bok Choy, diced
- 1 cup Chinese (Napa) cabbage, chopped
- ¼ cup fresh ginger, julienned

- 2 oyster mushrooms, sliced thin
- 1 cup green onions, chopped
- 4 oz. canned sliced water chestnuts, drained
- ½ red pepper, sliced thin
- 1 ½ cloves garlic, minced
- 1/8 to 1/16 teaspoon red pepper flakes (to taste)
- 1 cup snow peas
- ½ cup fresh bean sprouts
- 1 tablespoon soy sauce
- ¼ cup fresh cilantro, chopped
- 1 medium tomato, chopped

Directions:

1. Place Bok Choy, Chinese cabbage, ginger, mushrooms, green onions, water chestnuts, and red pepper in a large pot.
2. Add vegetable broth to the pot and bring to a boil.
3. Simmer covered over medium high heat for 5–10 minutes.
4. Add snow peas, tomato, and bean sprouts.
5. Simmer over medium heat for 5 minutes.
6. Add soy sauce and cilantro before serving.

Recipe makes 4 servings; 86 calories per serving.

Chicken Soup with Mushrooms

Ingredients:

- 4 cups chicken broth
- ½ teaspoon dried thyme
- 1 cup water
- 1 leek, stripped of outer shell, washed and sliced thin
- 6 oz. mushrooms, sliced
- 2 cups cooked boneless chicken breasts, chunked

- 8 oz. Brussels sprouts, quartered
- Dash of salt and pepper

Directions:

1. Combine chicken broth, thyme, and water in a large pot. Bring to a boil.
2. Add leek and mushrooms to the pot.
3. Simmer over low heat for 15 minutes.
4. Add chicken and Brussels sprouts to the pot.
5. Simmer over low heat for 6–7 minutes.
6. Add salt and pepper to taste.

Recipe makes 4 servings; 163 calories per serving.

Cream of Broccoli Soup

Ingredients:

- 1 tablespoon olive oil
- 1 onion, chopped
- 2 cloves garlic, minced
- 2 lb. broccoli, chopped
- Dash of salt and pepper
- 5 cups chicken broth, fat-free
- ¼ cup lemon juice

Directions:

1. Place olive oil in large nonstick saucepan and warm over medium heat.
2. Add onion and garlic to the saucepan and simmer for eight minutes.
3. Add broccoli, salt, and pepper to the saucepan and stir.
4. Add chicken broth and lemon juice and simmer two minutes.
5. Partially cover saucepan and simmer on low heat for 30 minutes.
6. Blend until you achieve a smooth, creamy texture.

Recipe makes 4 servings; 105 calories per serving.

High-Fiber Lentil Soup

Ingredients:

- 1 tablespoon olive oil
- 1 carrot, sliced thin
- 3 green onions, sliced thin
- 2 cloves garlic, minced

- 1 teaspoon chipotle chili powder
- 2 cups brown lentils, drained and rinsed
- 14 ½ oz. can diced tomatoes with juice
- 2 cups chicken broth
- 2 oz. lean ham, chopped

Directions:

1. Warm oil over medium heat in a large saucepan.
2. Add carrot to the saucepan and heat for five minutes.
3. Add scallions, garlic, and chili powder to the saucepan and heat for one minute.
4. Add lentils, tomatoes, broth, and ham to the saucepan and bring to a boil.
5. Simmer the saucepan mixture over low heat for 10–15 minutes.

Recipe makes 4 servings; 195 calories per serving.

Arugula Detoxification Soup

Ingredients:

- 1 tablespoon olive oil
- 1 onion, diced
- 1 clove garlic, sliced thin
- 2 cups broccoli

- 2 ½ cups water
- Dash of salt and pepper
- 1 cup arugula
- ½ lemon

Directions:

1. Pour olive oil into a nonstick saucepan and warm over medium heat.
2. Add onion and garlic to the saucepan. Simmer for two minutes.
3. Add broccoli to the saucepan and simmer for five minutes.
4. Add water, salt, and pepper to the saucepan and bring to a boil.
5. Simmer saucepan mixture over low heat for approximately 10 minutes.
6. Combine arugula and the saucepan mixture in a blender. Blend until it has a smooth consistency.
7. Squeeze fresh lemon juice over each bowl before serving.

Recipe makes 2 servings; 122 calories per serving.

Hearty Meatball Soup

Ingredients:

- 2 eggs
- ½ lb. lean ground beef
- 5 tablespoons bread crumbs
- ½ cup parsley, chopped
- Dash of salt and pepper
- 2 tablespoons olive oil, divided

- 2 cups onion, chopped
- 2 carrots, sliced thin
- 2 cloves garlic, chopped
- 8 cups escarole, rinsed, drained, shredded
- 5 cups chicken broth, low sodium

Directions:

1. Beat the eggs lightly.
2. Mix lean ground beef, bread crumbs, parsley, salt, pepper, and eggs in a large bowl. Mix well.
3. Scoop a tablespoon of the meat mixture at a time to form 24 meatballs.
4. Pour 1 tablespoon olive oil in a pot and warm over medium heat.
5. Place meatballs in the warmed pot. Flip over to ensure proper heating on all sides. Place warm meatballs on a plate or serving dish.
6. Add 1 tablespoon olive oil, onions, garlic, and carrots to the pot and heat for 10–15 minutes.
7. Add escarole to the pot and cook for five minutes.
8. Add meatballs and chicken broth to the pot and bring to a boil. Heat for an additional five minutes.

Recipe makes 6 servings; 187 calories per serving.

Quick and Easy Broccoli Soup

Ingredients:

- 2 cups broccoli, chopped
- 1 ½ cups chicken broth, low sodium
- 2 garlic cloves, minced
- 1 cup onion, chopped

- 1 tablespoon olive oil

Directions:

1. Simmer onion in olive oil until it becomes tender and light brown.
2. Add broccoli, chicken broth, and garlic.
3. Bring to a boil and then simmer for 15 minutes, covered, on medium heat.
4. Let the mixture cool and then process in a blender.
5. Add salt and pepper to your taste (just remember that the less salt, the healthier the soup will be).

Recipe makes 2 servings; 120 calories per serving.

Carrot and Rice Soup

Ingredients:

- 2 cups carrots, chopped
- 2 cups chicken broth, low sodium
- ½ cup long grain rice
- 2 tablespoons tomato paste

- 1 cup sweet onion, chopped
- 2 tablespoons olive oil

Directions:

1. Sauté onion with olive oil in a large saucepan until it has a light brown color.
2. Add carrot, chicken broth, tomato paste, and rice.
3. Bring to a boil and then simmer for 25 minutes, covered, on medium heat.
4. Let the mixture cool and then process soup in a blender.
5. Add salt and pepper to your taste (optional).

Recipe makes 2 servings; 160 calories per serving.

Cabbage Soup

Ingredients:

- 2 cups chicken broth
- 2 cups water
- ¼ medium cabbage head
- ½ cup chopped onion

- ½ cup celery, chopped
- ½ teaspoon ground pepper
- 2 medium tomatoes, chopped
- 1 bay leaf

Directions:

1. Mix chicken broth and water in a stockpot. Bring to boil and cook the cabbage, onion, and celery until tender.
2. Add pepper, tomatoes, bay leaf and simmer another 10 minutes.
3. Remove saucepan from heat and serve with dill on top.

Recipe makes 6 servings; 90 calories per serving.

Chicken and Noodles Soup

Ingredients:

- ½ lb. skinless chicken breast
- 1 chopped onion
- 2 carrots, chopped
- 2 garlic gloves

- 2 celery ribs, sliced
- 2 cups water
- 2 cups chicken broth, low sodium
- 3 oz. uncooked medium egg noodles
- 1/8 teaspoon ground pepper
- 1 tablespoon olive oil

Directions:

1. Pour olive oil in a large saucepan and sauté the chicken, garlic, and vegetables for 15 minutes.
2. Add broth, water, and pepper. Bring to a boil and simmer another 15 minutes, covered.
3. Add noodles and cook another 10 minutes or until noodles are tender.

Recipe makes 6 servings; 130 calories per serving.

Avocado and Cauliflower Soup

Ingredients:

- 2 avocados, peeled and pitted
- 2 cups chicken broth, low sodium
- 1 sweet onion, chopped
- 1 tablespoon lime juice
- 2 pinches of dried thyme

- 2 cups cauliflower, chopped
- 1 tablespoon olive oil

Directions:

1. Sauté onion with olive oil in a large saucepan until it has a light brown color.
2. Add cauliflower and cook another five minutes.
3. Add broth and bring to a boil.
4. Reduce heat and simmer about 20 minutes until cauliflower becomes soft.
5. Let soup cool.
6. Add avocado, lime juice and process in a blender until the mixture has a smooth texture.

Recipe makes 4 servings; 100 calories per serving.

Green Power Soup

Ingredients:

- 3 cups chopped spinach
- 2 medium zucchini, chopped
- 2 medium leeks, chopped
- 2 stalks of celery, chopped
- 2 cups chicken broth, low sodium

- 2 tablespoons basil
- 1 tablespoon olive oil
- 2 cloves garlic, minced

Directions:

1. Warm olive oil in a large saucepan over medium heat.
2. Add zucchini, leeks, celery, and garlic and simmer for 8 minutes.
3. Add 1 cup of broth and cook, stirring often, until vegetables are tender, about 10–15 minutes.
4. Process the soup in a blender and add basil.
5. Pour the soup back into the saucepan. Add 1 cup of broth and stir in the chopped spinach.
6. Cook another 5 minutes.
7. Add salt and pepper to your taste.

Recipe makes 3 servings; 137 calories per serving.

Tomato Soup

Ingredients:

- 1 can (28 oz.) diced tomatoes
- 2 medium onions, chopped
- ½ teaspoon brown sugar

- 1 tablespoon flour
- ¼ teaspoon baking soda
- 1 bay leaf
- 1 tablespoon butter
- 1 cup chicken broth, low sodium
- 1 tablespoon tomato paste
- ¼ cup "Half and Half", fat-free

Directions:

1. Melt the butter in a large saucepan and saute chopped onion until it has a light brown color.
2. Add tomatoes, sugar, and bay leaf. Cook about 10 minutes.
3. Add flour and tomato paste. Cook another 5 minutes.
4. Add chicken broth and baking soda and bring to a boil. Cook another 10 minutes.
5. Get rid of bay leaf and blend the soup by immersion blender.
6. Add "Half and Half", salt and pepper to your taste.

Recipe makes 4 servings; 166 calories per serving.

Smoky Corn Soup

Ingredients:

- 1 onion, chopped
- 2 cloves garlic
- 3 cups chicken broth
- ½ teaspoon smoke paprika

- ¼ teaspoon ground black pepper
- 50 ml "Half and Half"
- 8 oz. sweet corn
- 6 oz. potato, cut in cubes
- 1 tablespoon olive oil

Directions:

1. Cook onion garlic and potato in a saucepan with olive oil over medium heat for 5 minutes.
2. Add in pepper, garlic, and paprika.
3. Add corn, and broth. Bring to a boil and cook for 20 minutes.
4. Add the cream, put soup into a blender and puree until it has a smooth texture.
5. Return to the pot; add salt to your taste. Serve warm.

Recipe makes 6 servings; 164 calories per serving.

Cauliflower and Avocado Soup

Ingredients:

- 1 cup cauliflower, chopped
- 1 cup broccoli, chopped
- 1 sweet onion, chopped
- ¼ teaspoon smoked paprika

- ¼ teaspoon ground black pepper
- 1 avocado, pitted
- 3 cups chicken broth, low sodium
- ¼ teaspoon dried thyme
- 1 tablespoon olive oil

Directions:

1. In a large saucepan, sauté onion, garlic, and spices about 5 minutes over medium heat.
2. Add cauliflower and broccoli and cook another 5 minutes.
3. Add broth and bring to a boil.
4. Cover the pot and simmer for 20 minutes, until vegetables are soft.
5. Cool the soup, add avocado, and puree the mixture in a blender.
6. Serve warm. Put some parsley or dill leaves on top if desired.

Recipe makes 4 servings; 89 calories per serving.

Carrot and Ginger Soup

Ingredients:

- 4 medium carrots
- 1 medium butternut squash
- 1 onion, chopped
- 1 piece of ginger, 3 inches, sliced

- 3 cups chicken broth, low sodium
- ¼ teaspoon cinnamon
- 1 tablespoon olive oil
- 1 clove garlic, minced

Directions:

1. Bake butternut squash for half an hour in the oven at 350° F.
2. Let the squash cool and remove the skin.
3. Sauté onion and garlic in saucepan for 5–6 minutes over medium heat.
4. Add broth, carrots, ginger, and squash.
5. Bring to a boil and cook for half an hour.
6. Blend the mixture by immersion blender.
7. Heat the soup again. Add cinnamon, salt, and pepper to your taste.

Recipe makes 4 servings; 130 calories per serving.

Green Veggie Medley Soup

Ingredients:

- 2 cups cabbage (shredded)
- 2 cups broccoli (chopped)
- 2 medium carrots (chopped)
- 1 stalk celery (diced)
- 2 cups cauliflower
- 2 cups Swiss chard (chopped)
- 2 tbs. thyme (chopped)
- 2 cloves garlic
- 1 onion (chopped)

- 2 small zucchini (diced)
- 1 red bell pepper (diced)
- 2 tbs. parsley (chopped)
- 6 cups vegetable broth
- ½ fl. oz. lemon juice (optional)
- ½ tsp. table salt
- ¼ tsp. black pepper

Directions:

1. In a large pot, combine garlic, thyme, vegetables and the broth.

2. Bring the pot to a boil over high heat and cover. Lower the heat and let it simmer for about 10 minutes.

3. Add parsley, pepper, salt and lemon juice.

4. Let it simmer for a few more minutes and then serve.

Recipe makes 6 servings; 76 calories per serving.

Savory Tortilla Soup

Ingredients:

- 8 oz. corn tortillas cut into strips (1 package)
- 2 lb. skinless chicken breast cut into strips
- 2 limes (juiced)
- 28 oz. tomatoes (diced)
- 2 large onions (chopped)
- 8 cloves garlic (minced)
- 1 cup fresh cilantro (chopped)
- 12 cups reduced-sodium chicken broth
- 1 tbs. vegetable oil, reserve more for frying
- 1 tbs. coarse kosher salt
- ½ tsp. red chili flakes
- 1 tsp. ground cumin

- For toppings:
- Monterey jack cheese (grated)
- Avocado (sliced)
- Chopped cilantro
- Low fat sour cream
- Green onions (sliced/optional)

Directions:

1. In a large soup pot, heat 1 tbs. vegetable oil. Add onions and sauté for 5 to 7 minutes. Add 2/3 of the garlic, chili flakes, 1 tbs. salt, and cumin, then cook for another 2 minutes.
2. Put in the broth, half of the lime juice and tomatoes and cook for about 20 minutes.
3. In a separate frying pan, put the excess vegetable oil over medium high heat. Add 1/3 of the tortillas and cook until strips are golden brown. Prepare a pan with a paper towel and transfer the fried tortillas to it. Fry the remaining tortillas.
4. Use a blender to puree the soup in batches. Pour the soup back into the pot and allow it to simmer. Combine the chicken with the garlic, ½ tsp. salt and lime juice. Marinate it for about ten minutes, and then pour into the soup. Let it simmer for five minutes until chicken is tender. Add the cilantro. Serve with tortilla strips and your choice of toppings.
5. Recipe makes 10 servings; 192 calories per serving.

Gran's Lentil Soup

Ingredients:

- 2 carrots (peeled and sliced)
- 2 celery stalks (diced)
- 1 large onion (chopped)
- 2 large cloves garlic (minced)
- 1 large potato or 1 medium sweet potato (diced)
- 1¼ cups dried green or brown lentils

- 2 bay leaves
- 2 tsp. sweet paprika
- 16 oz. crushed tomatoes
- 2 tbs. extra virgin olive oil
- 1 tbs. salt-free all-purpose seasoning blend
- 6 cups water
- ¼ cup minced parsley or cilantro for toppings

Directions:

1. In a soup pot, sauté the onion over medium heat for about five minutes. Add the garlic, carrots, celery and cook for another 4 minutes.

2. Add water, lentils, potatoes, bay leaves, paprika and seasoning, then bring to a slow boil. Cover the pot and allow to simmer for about 30 minutes or until lentils and vegetables are visibly done.

3. Turn the stove to a low heat and add the tomatoes, cilantro and parsley to the mixture. Let it simmer for 15 minutes or until half of the lentils are gooey.

4. Season to taste by using salt and pepper. Let the soup stand for about an hour to improve the taste. Add toppings of choice before serving.

Recipe makes 6 servings; 171 calories per serving.

Light Roasted Red Pepper Soup

Ingredients:

- 8 red bell peppers (cut in half lengthwise)
- 5 black peppercorns
- 2 cups large onion (diced)
- 3 thyme sprigs
- 1 tbs. garlic (minced)
- ¼ tsp. freshly ground black pepper
- 1 bay leaf
- ¼ tsp. hot pepper sauce
- 4 cups less-sodium chicken broth
- 2 tsp. olive oil
- ½ tsp. salt
- 3 tbs. white wine vinegar
- 2 tbs. chives (chopped)

Directions:

1. Preheat broiler. Line the bell pepper halves on a baking sheet with the skin sides up, then flatten using the hand. Broil for 15 minutes or until darker in color. Keep sealed in a zip-top plastic bag for 15 minutes. Peel the pepper halves then chop.
2. Put the peppercorns, bay leaf, and thyme on a twofold cheesecloth. Tie the edges of the cheesecloth together.
3. Using a large Dutch oven, heat oil over medium heat. Sauté the onion and garlic until the onion is golden brown. Put the broth, vinegar, hot pepper sauce, bell peppers, and cheesecloth bag into the pan. Bring to a boil over medium-high heat. Decrease heat and cover the pan. Let it simmer for 20 minutes. Remove the cheesecloth bag then add salt and black pepper.
4. Mix half of the bell pepper using a blender. Eliminate the steam in the blender by removing the lid.
5. Put a clean towel on top of the opening of blender and allow mixture to blend until smooth.
6. Transfer the pureed mixture into a bowl and repeat the procedure with the remaining mixture. Garnish with chives.

Recipe makes 4 servings; 154 calories per serving.

Rich Tom Yum Soup

Ingredients:

- 2 ¼ inch slices galangal or ginger
- 4 Thai lime leaves/ 3 2-inch lime zest strips
- 1 ½ cups fresh pineapple (chopped)
- 1 tomato (chopped)
- ½ red bell pepper (cubed)
- 8 oz. raw shrimp (peeled)
- 2 jalapenos (sliced)
- 1 cup shiitake mushroom caps (sliced)
- 2 scallions (sliced)

- 1 stalk lemongrass (cut into one-inch pieces)
- 6 cups less-sodium chicken broth
- ¼ cup fresh lime juice
- 2 tbs. fish sauce
- 1 tsp. sugar
- 1/3 cup fresh cilantro (chopped)

Directions:

1. Beat the lemongrass and galangal on a chopping board using the side of a knife. Prepare a big saucepan and put in the smashed lemongrass, galangal (or ginger), jalapenos, lime leaves, and broth. Allow it to boil, then let it to simmer for 15 minutes.

2. Drain the mixture into a bowl and remove the solid ingredients.

3. Place the broth back into the saucepan together with the tomato, bell pepper, pineapple, mushrooms, sugar and fish sauce. Let it simmer while being uncovered for 5 minutes. Add the shrimp into the broth until the shrimp are thoroughly cooked.

4. Remove the mixture from heat and fold in the scallions, lime juice, and cilantro.

Recipe makes 5 servings; 125 calories per serving.

Classic Chicken Soup

Ingredients:

- 3 cups chicken breasts (diced)

- 8 cups chicken stock

- 1 medium carrot (chopped)

- 1½ cups celery (chopped)

- 1 cup onion (chopped)

- 1 tbs. olive oil

- 2 tbs. Italian seasoning

- 1 tsp. sea salt

- 1 tsp. pepper

Directions:

1. Season the chicken breasts with the salt and pepper. Place in a frying pan with oil until both sides are thoroughly cooked. Slice the cooked chicken breasts and place the slices back in the pan. Set aside.

2. Sauté onions, salt and pepper in olive oil using a stock pot for 3 to 4 minutes. Put the celery, carrots and Italian seasoning in the pot, and cook until the solid ingredients are tender.

3. Heat the chicken breasts in the frying pan and pour in a little bit of stock. Add the chicken breasts and stock to the vegetables.

4. Heat the remaining stock in a soup pot and cook over low heat for about an hour. Serve when hot.

Recipe makes 9 servings; 115 calories per serving.

Beets with Horseradish Borscht

Ingredients:

- 1½ cups steamed cubed beets, ½ inch sized cubes

- 1 medium russet potato (diced)

- ¼ medium cabbage head (chopped)

- 1 onion (chopped)

- 1 tbs. prepared horseradish

- 2 cups less-sodium beef or vegetable broth
- 2 tsp. red wine vinegar
- 2 tbs. extra virgin olive oil
- ¼ cup low-fat sour cream
- ¼ tsp. freshly ground pepper
- 1 tbs. parsley (chopped)

Directions:

1. Sauté onion in heated oil over medium heat for about 4 minutes or until brown. Add the potato, cabbage, broth, salt and pepper, and bring to a boil. Simmer over low heat, cover and let it cook until the potato is softened.

2. Add the beets and red wine vinegar and bring to a boil. Cover the saucepan and let it cook until the broth is red in color for about 3 more minutes.

3. Mix the horseradish and sour cream in a small bowl. Place a spoonful of the sour cream mixture onto the soup. Add parsley, then serve.

Recipe makes 4 servings; 180 calories per serving.

Tomato Spinach Delight

Ingredients:

- 15 oz. tomatoes (diced)
- 28 oz. tomatoes (crushed)
- ½ cup celery (chopped)
- 1 cup onion (chopped)
- 2 garlic cloves (chopped)
- 3 oz. fresh spinach (chopped)
- ¼ cup fresh basil (chopped)

- 1 tsp. dried oregano
- 1 tsp. dried thyme
- 1 freshly ground black pepper
- 1 tbs. balsamic vinegar
- 2 tsp. olive oil
- 2 cups low-sodium vegetable broth

Directions:

1. Using a Dutch oven or soup pot, heat oil and sauté garlic, onion and the celery until it is tender. Add a sprinkle of oregano and thyme while gently stirring.

2. Pour in the diced and canned tomatoes, vegetable broth, basil and spinach and cook until the vegetables are wilting.

3. Allow mixture to boil, then simmer over low heat for 15-20 minutes. Add balsamic vinegar and season with black pepper to taste.

Recipe makes 4 servings; 120 calories per serving.

Hot Vegetable Soup

Ingredients:

- ½ head small cabbage (cut into small strips)
- 6 green onions (sliced)
- 3 large carrots
- 2 green peppers (cut into bite seized pcs.)
- 6 stalks large celery
- 27 oz. tomatoes (canned)
- 10 oz. mushrooms (sliced)

- 2 cubes beef bouillon
- 6 cups vegetable juice
- 1 tsp. garlic powder
- 1 tsp red pepper flakes
- ½ tsp. salt
- 6 cups water

Directions:

1. Sauté green onions with cooking spray. Add the green pepper, cabbage leaves, and mushrooms. Sprinkle with a small amount of cayenne pepper.

2. Season the mixture using the beef bouillon, and then pour the water and vegetable juice. Cover and let it simmer over low heat.

3. Let it cook 20 minutes until cabbage is tender, then season the soup with salt and pepper.

Recipe makes 12 servings; 103 calories per serving.

Tofu Udon Soup

Ingredients:

- 1 pound extra-firm tofu (cut)

- 2 oz. dried Udon noodles

- 1 tbs. toasted sesame oil

- 1 tbs. soy sauce

- 6 cups low-sodium vegetable broth

- 10 oz. broccoli (chopped)

Directions:

1. In a mixing bowl, combine the tofu, soy sauce and toasted sesame oil. Set aside.

2. Pour the vegetable broth into a soup pot. Add broccoli, and Udon noodles. Bring to a boil and cook on medium heat.

3. Cover the pot and let it simmer for 5 minutes. Add the tofu mixture and stir gently.

Recipe makes 6 servings; 195 calories per serving.

Low Calorie Bloody Mary Soup

Ingredients:

- 1 large onion (diced)
- 3 ribs celery (chopped)
- 2 28-oz. cans whole tomatoes in juice (cut tomatoes into chunks)
- 2 tbs. unsalted butter
- 2 cloves garlic (minced)
- 2 tbs. Worcestershire sauce
- 2 tsp. horseradish (grated)
- Salt and pepper
- ¼ cup chilled heavy cream
- 3 tbs. chives (optional)
- 2 tsp. horseradish (grated)

Directions:

1. Melt unsalted butter in a soup pot over medium heat. Add the celery and onion and gently stir for 5 minutes until vegetables are tender. Add the garlic and sauté for about a minute, then fold in the Worcestershire sauce. Cook for another minute.

2. Add the tomato chunks and juice to the mixture and season with salt and pepper. Bring mixture to a boil then reduce to a simmer for about 20 minutes. Stir the mixture occasionally.

3. Remove mixture from heat, then add the horseradish. Let it stand for about 10 minutes, then puree the mixture in batches using a blender. Strain the mixture into a large pan and set aside.

4. Make the topping. Beat heavy cream with horseradish using an electric mixer until it forms stiff points. Serve the soup in a bowl and add a dollop of the cream mixture. Sprinkle with the chopped chives.

Recipe makes 8 servings; 96 calories per serving.

Mushroom and Barley Marmite

Ingredients:

- 1 cup raw pearl barley
- 10-12 oz. mushrooms (sliced)
- 1 onion (minced)
- 2 celery stalks (sliced)
- 3 carrots (sliced)
- Bay leaves
- 4 cups low-sodium vegetable stock plus 2 cups water
- 1 tbs. all-purpose seasoning mix
- 2 cups dairy-free milk
- ¼ cup parsley (minced)

- 2 tbs. fresh dill (minced)
- Salt and pepper

Directions:

1. Sauté onion in a stock pot. Pour in the vegetable stock and water, carrots, celery, bay leaves, barley, and seasoning. Let it boil and cover. Allow it to simmer for 25 to 30 minutes.

2. Add 1 cup of water and the mushrooms. Let it simmer for another 20 minutes until the vegetables are softened. Fold in dairy-free milk to allow the mixture to have a denser consistency.

3. Alter the taste of the mixture with condiments and add the dill and parsley. Remove the soup from heat and let it stand for about 30 minutes before serving.

Recipe makes 8 servings; 165 calories per serving.

Turkey Jerky Garlic Soup

Ingredients:

- 1 oz. turkey jerky (crumbled)

- 6 cups mustard greens

- 3 cups chicken broth

- 6 cloves garlic (crushed)

- 3 tbs. unfiltered apple cider vinegar

Directions:

1. Place the greens into a large soup pot and add the chicken broth. Cook over medium-low heat. Add the garlic, jerky, cayenne, and vinegar. Cover the mixture and stir occasionally for 10-15 minutes or until the greens are cooked.

2. Remove from heat and puree the mixture in a blender.

Recipe makes 4 servings; 64 calories per serving.

Northwestern Lentil Chili Soup

Ingredients:

- 1 cup dry lentils

- 1 cup carrots (diced)

- 1 potato (diced)

- 1 cup onion (diced)
- 1 clove garlic (minced)
- 2 tsp. chili powder
- 4 cups low-sodium V8
- 6 tbs. nonfat sour cream
- Olive oil cooking spray

Directions:

1. Spray a large pot with olive oil and heat over medium-high. Sauté garlic and onion for 2 to 3 minutes or until golden brown.

2. Add all the remaining ingredients and let it boil. Cover the mixture and let it simmer over low heat for about 20-30 minutes.

3. Remove from heat. Add a dollop of sour cream and chili on top of every serving.

Recipe makes 6 servings; 182 calories per serving.

Healthy Taco Soup

Ingredients:

- 2 cups tomatoes (crushed)
- 1 cup corn (drained)

- 2 cups chicken breasts (diced)
- 5 cups beans (canned)
- 8 oz. frozen spinach (chopped)
- 1 cup vegetable broth
- 1 packet of taco seasoning mix

Directions:

1. Season the chicken breasts with the salt and pepper. Place in a frying pan with oil until both sides are thoroughly cooked.

2. Combine all the ingredients in a large soup pot and season with taco seasoning mix. Cook over low heat 20 minutes.

3. Stir gently and remove from heat then serve. You can garnish the soup with jalapenos or nonfat sour cream.

Recipe makes 6 servings; 136 calories per serving.

Classic Eggplant Soup

Ingredients:

- 1 eggplant (peeled and cubed)

- 1 zucchini (peeled and cubed)

- 16 oz. tomatoes (stewed)
- 2 cloves garlic (chopped)
- 1 tsp. ground basil
- 1 tsp. ground oregano
- 1 tsp. ground thyme
- 1 tsp. salt and pepper
- 1 cup water

Directions:

1. Spray large soup pot with oil. Sauté the garlic, then add the zucchini and eggplant over medium heat. Cook until softened. Add tomatoes and pour in water and seasonings. Bring to a boil, then reduce heat.

2. Let it simmer uncovered for about 20 minutes to achieve preferred consistency. Remove from heat, then serve. You can pour it over brown rice or pasta if desired.

Recipe makes 4 servings; 69 calories per serving.

"Red Tide" Soup

Ingredients:

- 3 cups red bell pepper (roasted)

- 2 tbs. chopped garlic

- 1 cup of sliced yellow onions

- ¼ cup chopped basil

- 2 tbs. fresh thyme

- 3 cups vegetable stock

- 1 tsp. sea salt

- ½ tsp. black pepper

Directions:

1. Sauté garlic and onions until golden brown. Add bell peppers and vegetable stock. Bring to a boil. Then, reduce heat and let it simmer.

2. Season mixture using salt and pepper.

3. Remove from heat and let it warm for a few minutes. Fill blender with half of the mixture and blend until the desired consistency is achieved. Repeat the process with the remaining mixture.

4. Reheat all the blended soup then serve.

Recipe makes 4 servings; 85 calories per serving.

Chicken Asparagus Pottage

Ingredients:

- 2 cans asparagus pieces

- ¼ cup flour

- 2 tbsp. unsalted butter

- 4 cups stock (chicken)

- Onion (chopped)

Directions:

1. Melt unsalted butter in a soup pot over medium-to-high heat. Add flour and stir gently. Add onion and cook for about 3 minutes.

2. Pour in the asparagus and the chicken stock. Bring to a boil and then let it simmer for another 20 minutes.

3. Transfer the mixture into a food processor or blender by portions and puree. Season mixture with condiments. Serve hot.

Recipe makes 6 servings; 96 calories per serving.

Chicken-Parsnip Pea Soup

Ingredients:

- 1 cup parsnip (sliced diagonally)
- 1 cup shallots (sliced shallots)
- 1 cup skinless, boneless rotisserie chicken breast (shredded)
- 1 cup chickpeas (drained)
- 4 oz. packet of gourmet mushroom mix

- A clove of garlic (minced)
- 1 medium carrot
- 3 cups low-sodium chicken stock
- 1 thyme sprig
- 1 cup water
- 1½ tsp. olive oil
- ¼ tsp. salt
- ½ tsp. black pepper (freshly ground)
- 1/8 tsp. hot sauce
- 2 tbs. fresh parsley (chopped)

Directions:

1. Sauté garlic, mushrooms, shallots and parsnip in olive oil for 3 minutes.

2. Pour in broth and water, then add chickpeas, chicken breast, black pepper, salt, hot sauce and thyme sprig. Let it simmer for 10 to 12 minutes or until vegetables are soft.

3. Remove mixture from heat and garnish with parsley. Serve.

Recipe makes 6 servings; 154 calories per serving.

Green Velvet Pea Soup

Ingredients:

- 3 cups broccoli

- 3 cups spinach

- 1 cup dry split peas

- 3 zucchini (chopped)
- 1½ cup celery (chopped)
- 1 tbs. bay leaves
- 1½ cup yellow onion
- 1 clove garlic (minced)
- 1 cup potato flakes
- 12 cups water or broth

Directions:

1. Boil onion, garlic, celery, peas, and bay leaves in ½ of the water for an hour. Add the broccoli and spinach together with the remaining water and resume boiling until everything is softened.

2. Remove mixture from heat and puree in portions using a blender.

3. Add potatoes and season. Serve while hot.

Recipe makes 12 servings; 93 calories per serving.

Fresh Asparagus Chicken Soup

Ingredients:

- 14 oz. Asparagus

- 1 tbs. lemon juice

- 4 cups chicken stock

Directions:

1. In a soup pot, combine the chicken stock and fresh asparagus. Then, bring to a boil.

2. Add fresh lemon juice and wait until asparagus is wilted. Use an electric mixer to puree the mixture.

3. Season with pepper and serve.

Recipe makes 4 servings. 36 calories per serving.

Cool Pea and Mint Soup

Ingredients:

- 4 tbs. fresh mint (chopped)
- 10 oz. shelled young peas
- 1 medium potato (diced)
- 1 bunch spring onions (chopped)
- 1 clove garlic (crushed)
- Large pinch sugar

- 1 tbs. fresh lime juice
- 4 cups vegetable or chicken stock
- ½ cup buttermilk or soured cream

Directions:

1. Boil the spring onions, garlic, potato and stock in a large pan. Reduce the heat and let it simmer for 15 minutes or until the potato is tender.

2. Prepare the garnish. Boil 3 tablespoons of shelled peas in water for 2-3 minutes until blanched. Strain the peas and let it stand in a bowl of cold water.

3. Add the peas to the broth and let it simmer for 5 minutes. Stir in the sugar, mint, and lime juice. Let it cool for a few minutes, then transfer to a food processor and mix until smooth. Fold in half the buttermilk or soured cream, and season with salt and pepper.

4. Add more broth to the soup before serving as it thickens when it cools. Garnish the soup with the buttermilk and the peas.

Recipe makes 4 servings, 115 calories per serving.

Meatball Escarole Soup

Ingredients:

- 8 cups packed escarole (drained and shredded)
- ½ pounds lean ground beef
- 2 eggs (beaten)
- 6 tbs. Parmesan cheese (grated)
- 6 tbs. plain bread crumbs
- 2 cloves garlic (chopped)
- 2 onions (chopped)
- 2 carrots (sliced)
- 5 cups low-sodium chicken broth
- 2 tbs. olive oil

- 2 tsp. salt
- 1/8 tsp. black pepper
- ¼ cup fresh parsley (chopped)

Directions:

1. Place beef, 4 tbs. Parmesan cheese, parsley, pepper, salt, bread crumbs, and eggs in a large bowl. Mix and shape into 24 meatballs.

2. Heat oil in a stockpot over medium heat. Fry meatballs until all sides are browned. Set aside on a plate.

3. Cook the onions, garlic and carrots in the pot for 10 minutes or until vegetables are tender. Fold in escarole and cook for another 3 minutes. Add the broth and meatballs and bring to a boil.

4. Lower the heat and let it simmer for 5 minutes. Remove soup from heat and garnish with the remaining Parmesan cheese.

Recipe makes 6 servings; 198 calories per serving.

Homemade Tomato Gazpacho

Ingredients:

- 10 large tomatoes
- 1 large red pepper

- 2 cucumbers (peeled)//
- 6 cloves garlics
- 1/3 cup fresh coriander
- 5 tbs. wine vinegar
- ¼ cup olive oil
- 1 cup water

Directions:

1. Combine all ingredients in an electrical mixer or food processor. Add water until the consistency you desire is achieved.

2. Chill the mixture to let the flavors seep in before serving. Garnish soup with coriander or spring onions.

Recipes make 8 servings; 95 calories per serving.

Spicy Soup: "Aunt Love"

Finally, here is my favorite soup recipe from my dear friend Aunt Love. It is an extremely easy and extremely delicious soup. Prepare all ingredients separately and then mix them to your taste.

Ingredients:

- 1 whole chicken
- 1 medium head of white cabbage
- 2 bay leaves

- 1 teaspoon red pepper
- 5 cloves garlic, minced
- 1 lb. whole wheat home style noodles (choose noodles with as low calories as possible)
- 1/2 teaspoon salt
- 2 medium onions
- ¼ teaspoon black ground pepper
- 1 tablespoon olive oil

Directions:

1. Put the chicken carcass in a big pot with water and bring it to a boil.
2. Reduce the heat. Add bay leaves, fresh ground pepper, and 2 whole, peeled onions. Cook about 30 minutes.
3. When the chicken is cooked, remove it from the broth, separate the meat from the bones, cut meat into small pieces, and set it apart. This is your first ingredient.
4. Take bay leaves and onions out of the broth. This wonderful chicken broth is your second ingredient.
5. Add pasta into another big pot of boiling water. Cook for 7-10 minutes. Drain, rinse with cold water and drain again. Add 1 teaspoon of olive oil and mix well. This is your third ingredient.
6. The fourth and most important ingredient is spicy cabbage. Put the chopped cabbage into a large bowl. Add salt, mix well, and leave it for 15

minutes, so cabbage begins to give juice. Then put the cabbage in a colander and squeeze well to remove the juice.
7. Put squeezed cabbage into a large saucepan with 1 tablespoon olive oil. Add garlic and red pepper. Saute over medium heat for 15 minutes, stirring occasionally.
8. For one serving, put into the soup bowl ½ cup of noodles, ¼ cup of chicken meat, ¼ cup of spicy cabbage, and 1 ½ cup of hot chicken broth. You can vary the proportions based on your personal preferences.

The recipe gives you ingredients for about 10 servings with about 171 calories per serving.

Please be advised that soup's caloric value really depends on the ingredients and brands you are using and could be drastically variable. Keep a close eye on that value. I recommend finding a dependable online calorie calculator (there are many apps available for this purpose) and carefully calculating your daily caloric intake.

From the Author.

I'm a mother and a writer. I love my children, my home, my garden and my kitchen. I'm also a big enthusiast of healthy food. I love to grow it, cook it and write about it.

Thank you for purchasing my book. I hope you enjoyed nutritional soup recipes. If this book was beneficial for your health and fitness goals, please leave a couple of friendly words at the Amazon book page.

You may also consider reading other books from my series "Healthy Cooking for Healthy Living"

Juicing for Health

Juicing
for Health

Julia Cussler

Quick and Easy Soup Recipes

Vegetarian Slow Cooker Recipes

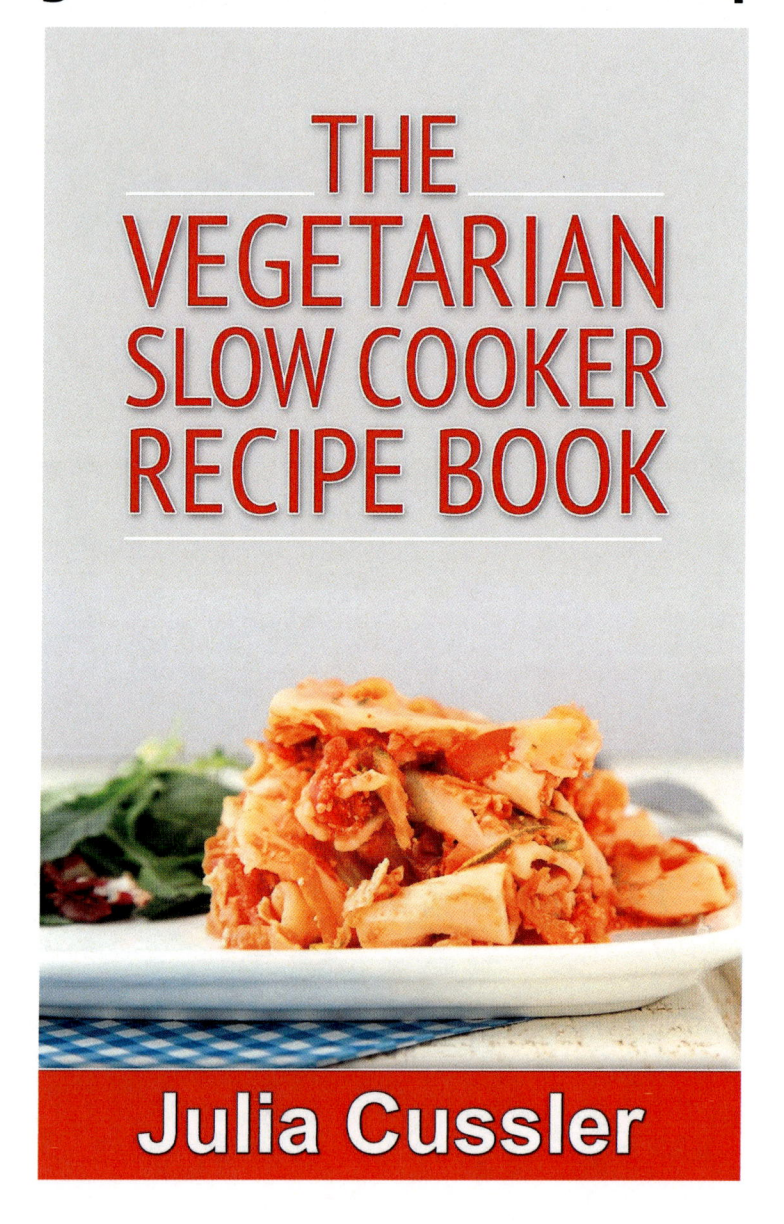

THE VEGETARIAN SLOW COOKER RECIPE BOOK

Julia Cussler

Natural Cholesterol Solution

Juicing
Natural Cholesterol Solution

Julia Cussler

Please visit my Vegetable Gardening blog **veggrowing.com**. You will learn how to effectively grow your own organic produce for healthy cooking and juicing.

I wish you good luck on your route to healthy life!

Made in the USA
Middletown, DE
13 June 2023